ALL MIRACLE

Packages

To my dear
friends in
Christ,
Win and Bob,
with love
always,
Patti

April 9, 1924–February 16, 1999

ALL MIRACLE

*P*ackages

Poems by
Elizabeth B. Rooney

Edited by
Patricia M. Rooney

Brigham Farm
Publishing

Published by Brigham Farm Publishing
2990 Cave of the Mounds Road
Blue Mounds, WI 53517
www.brighamfarm.com

Cover photograph © 1998 Marilyn Collins. For more
information about photographs by this artist, e-mail her
at www.wndsng1.com or write to WindSong Photography,
6425 Shenandoah Way, Madison, WI 53705.

Interior artwork © 2001 Simone Portia McLoughlin

Cover and book design by Elizabeth Ragsdale

Quote by Luci Shaw in preface is used with permission of
the author.

Library of Congress Control Number: 2001119945

ISBN 0-9716001-0-4 (set of four)
ISBN 0-9716001-1-2 (v. 1)
ISBN 0-9716001-2-0 (v. 2)
ISBN 0-9716001-3-9 (v. 3)
ISBN 0-9716001-4-7 (v. 4)

To my wonderful family—
Dad; Mark and Gail;
Jon; Betsy and Doug;
David, Timmy, and Adam.

ALL MIRACLE SERIES

Elizabeth B. Rooney

Morning Song

Packages

Storing September

Gift Wrapped

Contents

June

July

August

Preface

This series of books is for all of Elizabeth Rooney's family, friends and fans who have been patiently awaiting the publication of her collected poems and for all those who will meet her for the first time in these pages.

Elizabeth Brigham Rooney, my mother, began writing poems in the summer of 1978. Before her death in February 1999, she had written over seven hundred of them, interspersed amongst the prose entries in her journals like bursts of song.

She was more surprised than anyone at this sudden and abundant release of creativity, although she'd been encouraged from her youth to pursue a career in writing. Raised by highly literate parents, she attended and excelled at top-notch schools, yet protested, "I don't have anything to say!"

Later, she came to realize the creative flow had been blocked, among other things, by fear of failing those who expected so much from her. It wasn't until she made a complete surrender to the One who had placed the love of poetry inside her that she was free, not only to write but also to embrace all of life as a holy gift.

This "total commitment," as she described it, came as she was preparing to be inducted into the Society of the Companions of the Holy Cross, a lay order of Episcopal women. She already had her masters in Christian Education and was married to an Episcopal priest, yet there was something missing.

"For years I'd been an active Christian adult and before that, a rather timid, but believing child. I prayed quite regularly for as long as I can remember, but at the same time stayed a safe distance from the cross. To embrace the cross wholeheartedly requires an act of will. To my astonishment, the result was an absolute flooding of joy. I had fallen in love with God. It was as if my veins were bubbling with champagne and the poems began to flow freely, coming as delightful surprises day after day."

The first one to come was "Adelynrood," named for the retreat center in Massachusetts where the encounter took place.

Adelynrood

The winter of my heart
Melts here.
Rivulets run
Beneath the ice of fear.

Pierced by your warmth,
Life moves.
Spring has begun.
I feel the sun, the sun!

8/11/78

As her newly awakened faith grew, so did the conviction that these poems were gifts to be shared. She summoned the courage to exchange poetry with friends who were fellow writers. Then she attended a workshop led by the poet Luci Shaw and there found a kindred heart and mind, a friend and mentor, who eventually introduced her to the reading public in a way Elizabeth never dreamed possible.

Luci had been asked to write a chapter in an upcoming book entitled *Bright Legacy, Portraits of Ten Outstanding Christian Women* about someone she "particularly admired." As Luci explains in her chapter, "Rather then telling of the impact on my life of an internationally known personality, I felt a growing conviction that I would rather talk about someone like Elizabeth Rooney, an 'ordinary' woman, hardly known beyond her own circle of friends and colleagues, though uniquely gifted by God. Her experience would, I was sure, suggest to other women with earthbound, unremarkable lives that he could lift the most mundane existence into his own bright beauty and glory. What he requires are eyes open to his brightness and ears alert for his voice."

Luci's words so aptly describe the gift Elizabeth received at Adelynrood. She had indeed been given "eyes open to his brightness and ears alert for his voice." And so the woman who had protested she had nothing to write about, was able to declare, "I know what I want to say. . . . I want to write about God, about the intense tenderness manifest in the world wherever goodness, truth and beauty allow it to shine through… Today in the parking lot there was a puddle—a muddy, shallow puddle on the blacktop, not more than an inch deep at best and perhaps four feet across. When looked at from a certain angle, it reflected all the treetops in it, and clouds and sky, all the way to infinity. I think I'm like the puddle—muddy, shallow, insignificant—but, by God's grace, capable of the miracle of reflecting him, and in him, all the wonder of the universe.

"The more I become aware of the active presence of God, the more beautiful and sacred everything becomes. . . . Do we need miracles, or do we need only to perceive that every ordinary thing around us is already miraculous?"

My mother's hope, as voiced in the following prayer by an unknown author, was that her poems might open other eyes to His brightness and other ears to His voice, that they would come to understand as she had that "Life is *all* miracle."

"Days pass and the years vanish and we walk sightless among miracles. Lord, fill our eyes with seeing and our minds with knowing. Let there be moments when your Presence, like lightning, illumines the darkness in which we walk. Help us to see, wherever we gaze, that the bush burns unconsumed. And we, clay touched by God, will reach out for holiness and exclaim in wonder, 'How filled with awe is this place and we did not know it.'"

« »

This series, *All Miracle*, includes four volumes, *Morning Song*, *Packages*, *Storing September*, and *Gift Wrapped*, which correspond to spring, summer, autumn, and winter. Those who, like my mother, have grown up on farms or in the country understand and interpret life, in large part, by the passage of the seasons. Her poetry is characterized by a deep awareness of life's interconnectedness and the yearly cycles of death and rebirth. After much reading and rereading of the poems, I felt the most natural way to group them would be by these intrinsic themes, which include not only the four seasons but also the parallel seasons of human life, such as childhood, adulthood, aging, and death and the corresponding seasons of the liturgical year, such as Advent, Christmas, Lent, and Easter. Although each poem is meant to be read and savored on its own, the groupings are intended to accentuate their collective rhythm and flow.

—*Patricia M. Rooney*

Acknowledgments

My most sincere thanks to the following persons and companies:

To all who helped launch this publishing venture by generously contributing to the Elizabeth B. Rooney Memorial Poetry Fund.

To Eugenia Brown, who so cheerfully volunteered hours and hours of typing.

To Louise Summers, Delores Topliff, Pat Hitchcock, Norma Madsen, Sharol Hayner, Joyce Young, Kimberly Linyard, Janice Griffin, and Sr. Peronne-Marie Thiebert, for their gracious help with proofreading.

To my brother Mark, for all of his encouragement, advice, and nagging.

To the wonderful folks at Impressions Book and Journal Services, Inc., especially John Ferguson, Mary Boss, and Elizabeth Ragsdale, for their expertise, enthusiasm, and genuine interest in this project. Your patience and warmth working with a first-time publisher made all the difference.

To Kevin Wasowski and Jane Landen of Edwards Brothers, for their kind and professional help.

Summer

I love late June is Wisconsin. The corn is about two feel tall and the leaves glisten and shine. The oats are almost ready to head out, the stalks are a deep blue-green. Farmers are presently in the midst of hay-making, so that many fields are lined with rich sweet smelling swaths of drying alfalfa . . . the strawberries are ripe, lettuce and spinach are all in, and the rest of the garden looks tidy and promising. Yes, there is a sweetness to early summer, a time of beauty and hope.

Journal, 6/6/78

*P*ackages

If I could wrap
A field of butterflies,
I'd package them
For you.
I'd put in all the colors
And a lot of sunshine, too.
I'd gather up a summer breeze
And all the fluttering
And wrap them with brown paper
And tie them up with string.

I've only words for wrapping
And only rhymes for string.
With these, beloved of my heart,
I give you everything.

1/15/87

June

Reading Lesson

What shall I write, my Lord?
Write about me.
What shall I tell them, Lord?
Tell them how beautiful I am.

But that's been written already, Lord.
In the sky,
In the pine needles under my feet,
In granite and sand,
In all of the sparkle and shine
Of your world.

I know, child,
I wrote the book.
Tell them to look.

9/20/79

Angels

Wings beat above the world!
Swift-wing'd here,
Hummingbird swoops and swirls,
And finches flutter
Around the rowan berries.

In feather-fluted tune,
Each wingbeat carries
Echoes of other wings,
Of other worlds.

8/11/78

Fire Flower

(Dedicated to orange tiger lilies)

The bush burned once,
But you burn every year.
Scarlet and orange
Blaze above your green,
Miraculous as fire
That leaves entire
And unconsumed
The branches where it feeds.

Ah, had we hearts to see,
We would not pass you by,
Would rather stand and stare,
Our busyness unshod,
Shocked by your flaming wonder
And aware
That all the universe
Is filled with God.

7/29/79

Eschaton

I saw the world end yesterday!
A flight of angels tore
Its cover off and Heaven lay
Where earth had been before.

I walked about the countryside
And saw a cricket pass.
Then, bending closer, I espied
An ecstasy of grass.

8/17/78

Significance

Hope, in a muddy flower,
Infinity, caught in a shallow pool,
Eternity, in every passing hour,
And You, creator God, in every fool.

We have our worth,
Each one, our dignity,
Our minute place,
Yet we are real
Only through your benignity
And by permission of your grace.

3/10/79

Simple

As simple as a seamless robe,
The total texture of the life
Woven into one single, simple piece.
A seamless robe is woven whole—
Nothing subtracted, nothing added on.
Then, wholly given to God
That He may move
Within the fabric of our universe.

Is it all seamless—
Every bird and leaf,
The dailyness, the ecstasy, the grief—
All interwoven in one holy whole?
Yes, all is whole cloth,
All, one sheet of fire,
All, undivided as the flame
That animates the air—
Not just at Pentecost,
But everywhere.

7/22/80

Persistent

Once, very quietly, Love came
As baby, innocent and mild.
But we? We killed the Holy Child.
Then was Love true to Love.
For all that we could do,
He stayed the same.
He did not hate us for his death.
Again, He came—
This time
As living breath of flame.

12/22/80

Miracles

I hold within my hand
Infinities I cannot comprehend—
Worlds within wonder worlds.
Sometimes, a blade of grass . . .
Again, a clover leaf,
A bit of bark, a bug
Minute and unidentifiable.
I touch them reverently
And wonder how God made it all—
Our world, our universe
So huge, so small.

4/30/88

Carpenter

Jesus, Jesus,
Carpenter of Nazareth,
Can you make a lintel?
Can you make a door?

Jesus, Jesus,
Carpenter of Nazareth,
Can you make a universe
Where there was none before?

Jesus, Jesus,
Carpenter of Nazareth,
Living in the midst of us,
A working man and poor,

How shall we esteem you,
Holy, humble carpenter?
By the universe you made—
And also by the door.

6/28/82

Profligate

One dandelion
Would suffice
For those
Whose measurements are nice.
One leaf
In its perfection
Be enough.
Who needs a maple tree?

But God can't have too much
Of trees,
Stars, snowflakes, dandelions,
Bees.
He's always
Making more and more.
He inundates us
With His store
Of sheer, creative energy.

Oh, praise Him
For all things that be!

5/22/87

✳ *Creator*

And on the seventh day,
The day He rested
And looked at all He'd made
And called it good,
Did God rejoice in snowflakes falling softly,
Did He watch a wave's edge curl across the sand,
Did He see the power of the oak within an acorn,
Did He touch the fine green mosses with His hand?

Of course, He did,
He who had dreamed and fashioned
All of the intricacy of our earth.
He loved, He loves and He will love forever
Every least particle to which His Word gave birth.

3/21/93

Big and Little

Creator of the splendor of the skies,
Thank You for bothering
To make fireflies.
After You lit the moon
That lights the night
And got the planets
Orbiting just right,
Did You look down on earth
And laugh and shrug
And make the lightning bug?

7/11/93

Snail's Lament

Creator God,
You made me snail,
Helpless and soft
All eyes and tail.
Your love designed me
Small and slow.
Dear God,
With all the possibilities at Your command
Why did you make me so?

9/19/93

Revelation

Having been brought up to treat
Holy things with reverence sweet,
I grow gentler as I find
Each thing holy of its kind.

1/24/94

Remembering

I held a swallow once
Within my hand
And felt the sweet life
Trembling in the bones.
It was so swift,
So delicate, so strong—
A magic creature
Made of wings and song—
And yet so vulnerable
In my palm.

When it was warmed
And soothed,
At peace and calm,
I let it go
Back to the open sky
From which it came.
Now all the sky
Sings for me,
And the hollow of my hand
Will never be the same.

10/28/88

On Journey

Go quietly
Along the road of love.
Leave only feather footfalls
In the grass.

Bruise nothing, no one
Of the tender green
Clinging about you
As you seek to pass.

8/15/78

Almost Eden

Mine is a green and singing world,
Where small, furred creatures
Move about at night.
They sleep now
With the coming of the light
And let me have my turn
At living with the clover in the lawn,
The butterflies,
The bean rows in the garden,
The high summer skies.
We share this miracle of green
God's given us,
But sometimes, when they eat the beans,
I fuss.

6/27/92

Summer Breeze

The breeze is bright with butterflies.
I hadn't meant to stay
So long here by the roadside
Where the prairie flowers sway.
But, oh, dear Lord of beauty,
How can I go away
When every breeze is summer bright
With butterflies today?

7/30/86

Sanctuary

My altar is the forest floor.
My altar flowers are trees.
For candles, I have sun and moon.
What handsomer than these?

The song birds are the choristers.
Thy Presence, bread and wine.
The whole world is Thy chalice, Lord.
Help us to know it Thine.

6/8/79

Reminder

Lord, let there be a window
Over every kitchen sink
So, when our hands are busy,
We can think
Of trees and grass and sky
And thus, of You
And feel Your love
When light comes shining through.

10/24/87

Love Song

Today my poem will be written
Not in words
But in the work I do
To make the house
Shining and welcoming.

Today my poem will be written
Not with pen
But with my mop and broom,
With clean sheets,
With my iron and paring knife.

A love song, yes—
One written with my life.

8/24/88

Circle of Love

I am in love
With the little things of life—
A small white dog,
A birch tree in the sun,
Two gold finches,
The smell of dinner
Nearly done.

I live within
The circle of our love,
Not big
But big enough
To hold two hearts in tune.
Will you be coming soon?

9/3/80

Wedding Prayer

Lord of our lives,
We ask that You will take
The singleness of each of us
And make of us
A being altogether new,
A marriage,
Forming one flesh
Of our two.

Take the plain water
Of our daily life
And bless it
So we may become such wine
That all who drink
Will taste in our love,
Thine.

5/26/86

Wedding Hymn

You are the gift He's given
For my wanting.
You're the still waters
I lie down beside.
You're the green pastures
Where I take my pleasure.
You are my own beloved joy,
My pride.

Through your sweet love
He has restored my wholeness.
He fills my shadowed valley
With your light.
You are the staff
With which He holds my weakness.
You are the feast
He sets for my delight.

Yours is the love
With which His love anoints me.
You are His overflowing
Cup of grace.
Through you,
His goodness and His love
Surround me.
In you,
I come at last
To see His face.

6/11/87

Wedding Guest

They stand together on the grass,
Suddenly shy and shining.
We hear them speak
The promises of love
And seek
In their bright hope
Assurance that our own
Past promises
Are not outgrown.

Now in and through
Their joining
Flow the streams
Of all our lives,
Though none quite what it seems.
Are the tears in our eyes
For their young love
Or for our own lost dreams?

5/16/81

Nest Builders

Like birds,
We wove the pieces carefully,
Sought out a place sheltered and strong
And worked together
Fetching sticks and grass.
How frail and yet how firm
Our little nest
Woven of love, of sacrifice, of trust.
So many conflicts, struggles, strains,
Such buffeting from wind and rains,
And yet, we held, we stayed
So that the nestlings from the eggs we'd laid
Could shelter safely
Till their wings were strong,
Till they would fill the air
With their bright flight and song.

1/2/94

Homespun

You are my husbandman
And I am wife.
We are the warp and woof
Of one another's life.
Enmeshed within the pattern
Of our days,
We are too interwoven,
Love, to see
The tapestry God makes
Of you and me.

12/13/78

Daily News

Our tissue paper hearts
Lie neatly folded on the sill of day.
We will unfold them when you come
And read each other all the great events.
I will smooth out your wrinkles
And you, mine,
So we can see more clearly line by line.
Then, after we have read each other through,
We will be made all virginal and new,
Ready to be imprinted once again
With joy and tedium and love and pain.

1/22/79

To One Long Married

Beloved, since I've had you,
Have I ever let you fly,
Float free
Beyond the limits
And the narrowness of me?

Have you ever wished
That you could run away
And be your own, unfettered self
For just a day?

Now, while we still have time,
Let's try
To recognize the wishes deep
Within one another's hearts
And free each other's dreams
To fly.

9/12/95

Morning Light

Perhaps the light in heaven
Will be like
The light on a June morning
Where it comes
Slanting across the fields,
Gilding the green
And shoots straight through
The window facing east.

Released within the room
It penetrates
The green shirt
Hanging from a bureau drawer,
The socks and loafers
Heaped upon the floor.
Everything gleams with gold,
Transformed
As we shall be
When morning comes for us
And God's great love
Illuminates our souls
And sets us free.

6/12/94

Always

Always
Is not too often
To give praise
To this most loving God of ours
Who fills His days
With blessing us
And making all things good.
Nor do we praise Him
Just because we should
But rather because everywhere we turn
We cannot but discern
His seeking, caring love
Surrounding us.
All praise, all glory and all honor be
To God—now, always and eternally!

1/24/88

July

Summer

Summer is for remembering—
For feeling wet grass cool beneath your feet,
For sitting on the porch and shelling peas,
For strawberries,
For hearing screen doors slam,
For drinking lemonade so sour sweet
The taste explodes in your throat
Like the Fourth of July.

Summer is sky,
Sky wheeling with fireworks,
Sky when the stars come down
And flicker on and off among the trees,
Sky full of tasseling corn,
Sky interlaced with feathered heads of grass
When you lie on your back
To watch the high clouds pass.

Summer is coming home from the pool
With your clothes damp on your skin
And your body, cool.
Summer is hammocks and picnics and croquet
And, even after summer goes away,
Summer is for remembering.

7/25/80

Making Bee Hives

The air is sweet with sap and honey,
As the old man draws his plane along the wood.
A breeze moves creamy curls across the floor.
They lie tangled in every corner.
Sunlight filters through wood dust
And the dust of the bodies of the bees.
The world outside is alive,
Crossed by the flight paths of a million messengers.
I am long ago,
A child on a high stool in the corner
Overcome by the flower fragrance of pollen.

3/1/79

Family Reunion

When I step on the porch,
Feet other than mine
Go with me.
For I have stepped
On this porch before,
Was once a baby
Crawling on this floor.
Remembered footsteps
Echo in my ears,
Reverberate
Through more than fifty years
Of stepping on this porch,
Closing this door,
Walking across this floor.
However quietly I go,
They are all around me.
Here on this porch
The people of my past
Surround me.

6/8/81

Roots

Unlike so many Americans
Whose pasts have become
Apartment parking lots,
I sleep each night
In the room where I was conceived.
I can remember
Other shoes in the closet,
Other shapes in the bed.
Is it safe to dream
In this room
Or will the shapes of my childhood
Overwhelm today?

I am deep-rooted here—
The child who sat at this window long ago,
One with the child who lives within me now.
I do not wish either to hoard
Or throw away this past—
Simple to be,
Here in the present,
Aware of its working in me.

Train Whistle

I hear it in the night
Years afterward,
A long, low trumpet call
Far, far away.

I was only a child
Hunched at the window,
Looking at the moon,
Imagining
What I would do some day,
When I first heard
Its low, deep-throated call.

It made me want
To conquer some distant world,
Where there were streets
And skyscrapers
And power.

I still remember the thrill
And the pull of it,
As if I heard it
Just within the hour.

11/20/87

Brother

You've always been there.
You are one of the boundaries
Of the property
I call myself.
I've always been defined
In part
By my relationship to you.
I was your sister
Years before I knew
Who else I was.
And you're the only person
Who remembers
All of the little things.

Yes, we've grown up,
We've lived our separate lives.
And yet, I've always known
That you were there.
So, while we still have time,
I thought I'd let you know
I care.

3/1/88

Church

I remember being a child
In a country church—
Kneeling against the hard slats of our pew,
Turning my back on the minister
To view the faces of the people
Who had come
To sit in this quiet place.
I had no idea
Of the trouble they brought to the Lord,
Of their doubts or their grief.
But even a child
Could feel their sense of relief
From cares, from whatever sorrow
They could lay down for a while
But would carry tomorrow.
We prayed and we listened to prayer,
The smell of alfalfa
Came in on the summer air—
And God was there.

Blue Mounds

Even if I were dead,
I would remember this hill—
The view in the morning mists,
The thrill
Of the first snow flake in the fall,
The first pasque flower in spring,
The cinnamon coloring
Of the leaf-covered ground
In November.
Even if I were dead,
I would remember.

11/25/80

Grandson

I would like
To have imprinted in him here
The quiet of this place,
So that the murmur of the leaves
Lives on in him,
So that he carries
Deep within his soul
The feeling of breeze against his cheek,
And the way it lifts his hair.
I would have him remember the porch
And the singing of wrens,
The oak tree that lights like a torch
When the long summer ends.
I would have him remember the skies
And the butterflies.

6/12/92

Emma Lou

They gave her a name
Like a country town
To call from the porch
As the sun goes down—
Emma Lou, Emma Lou!

They gave her a name
Like a gingham gown,
A name to wear
When the boys come roun'—
Emma Lou, Emma Lou!

She took her name
And she traveled far,
Studied and taught
And became a star—
Emma Lou, Emma Lou!

But still at night
As the sun goes down,
She hears them call
In the little town
The name that sounds
Like a gingham gown—
Emma Lou, Emma Lou!

9/15/84

Collection

The orioles' nest remembers
The flashing orange
And the pale green worm,
The warbling whistles
High in the misted leaves.
The shell remembers the sea,
The vertical, tumbling,
Green-blue wall of it.
The butterfly wing remembers
Falling and fluttering
Through spring sky
And the touch of petals.
My heart remembers you—
Remembers and remembers.

4/26/79

Long Neck Point

A place of singing birds
Beside the shore
Where sea gulls' cry
Mingles with the soft mourning
Of the doves,
Where tulip trees
Drop their cupped yellow blossoms
From the sky,
Where every breeze
Carries the scents
Of marsh and salt and sea—
This is the gracious place
That welcomes me,
This is the place I love.

5/30/91

Morning in the North

Mist rises on the lake.
In clammy clothes
We tiptoe toward the shore.
Stealthily launched,
We lift our paddles,
Feathering them softly.
We drift in a world of ghosts.
A loon calls
And a beaver slaps his tail.
We glide in stillness
Over liquid stillness.
Later, there will be sunshine and splashing.
Now, all is misted magic.

3/4/79

Attuned

You murmur within
And around me.
As surf-sound penetrates
The cottage at the shore,
Pine-sound, the cabin
In the northern woods,
So, your sound
Penetrates
My very soul.
The deepest core of me
Reverberates
And resonates with you.
You sing, you weep, you laugh
And I am
Singing, weeping, laughing too.

4/27/88

My Friend

You are a wide, warm place
Within my soul,
A clearing in life's wood,
A sun-drenched glade.
I sit among the summer sweetness of you
Or lie back,
Half asleep upon the grass.
Your quiet warmth,
Your welcoming affection
Support me like the steadiness of earth.
Through the long afternoon,
Our words rustle above me.
Reluctantly, I leave.
When I get home,
I find that I am healed.

1/2/79

Jane

There was about you always
A quality of silver.
You reminded me of bells,
Of something shimmering,
Like breeze-blown catkins
Or the glistening path
That moonlight makes on water.

Now that you've let me see
So much of the reality of you—
All the plain human needs,
The struggle and the courage
And the longing—
You are even more perfectly
Silver to me,
Purer from life's refining,
Sudden and quick and shining.

4/12/88

Treasure

You are my eagle's egg,
My special curving shell,
My spotted stone
Whose hollow fits my thumb,
My monarch wing,
My faded maple leaf.

When I uphold you
To our Lord in prayer,
I spread before Him there
The childhood of my heart.

An offering
Of foolish fondness, this—
And yet, to offer it
Is very bliss.

4/26/79

Affirmation

If you were a silver bowl,
I'd polish you
And fill you with bright fruit
And set you high
So people could see you shine
As they walked by.

If you were a brand-new foal,
I'd rub you with clean straw
And brush your coat all bright
And leave you in the sun
So people could delight.

If you were a sapling,
Green and slender,
With new spring leaves
All moist and tender,
I'd shelter you from worm and canker
Until your springing roots found anchor.

I'd love you, tend you, set you free
From all that binds,
Including me,
So you could praise God gloriously.

5/23/84

My Friend

You let me walk around your heart
Purring and velveted.
Imprisoned
In the freedom of your love,
I yawn and stretch and sleep
And wake to find
That you are still my keeper
And still kind.

11/17/78

Return

When the corn is green
And the oats are blue,
When the ground fog
Covers the morning view,
I will come to you,
I will come to you.

When the ribboned fields
Gleam halfway high,
And the fresh cut hay
Smells sweet and dry,
I will come to you,
I will come to you.

When the cows in the marsh
Stand belly deep,
And the new fawns
Curl in the shade to sleep,
I will come to you,
I will come to you.

When the swallows fly
Through the old shed door,
And my heart returns
To the farm once more,
I will come to you,
I will come to you.

7/12/82

Circle of Friends

Of course, we meet!
We meet within your heart,
And gathered in the circle of your love
We greet each other fondly
And begin that interchange
Of thought and joke and prayer
That knits us each to each.
No matter that our lives are lived apart.
You reach across the miles
And by your love
Unite us in your heart.

7/10/96

Invitation

Good morning, stranger!
Will you be my friend?
Will you and I begin
The tentative approaches
And retreats
Through which one gradually meets
Another soul?
Dare we exchange
Nods, smiles, small pieces of ourselves,
Till we grow bold enough to share
The secrets of our hearts,
The needs, the griefs
We bring to God in prayer?
Come, stranger-friend,
Let us begin at least to chance
The delicate maneuvers
Of this dance.

4/18/92

Greeting

Our rising souls rush out to meet,
So eager to embrace
We have no thought
Of putting on a tidy morning face.

So each encounters each
As bare of ornament or plan
As lovers met in Eden
Before consciousness began.

4/14/79

Fine Line

For all of us,
Life is precarious.
We walk along
The edges of despair.
Some get so near the edge
They freeze in fear
And some
Fall
Screaming...

Most of us
Are not there,
But we are near.
We know
How much we need
Families and friends,
Forgiveness,
Love and grace,
If we are to maintain
A steady, Godward pace

6/6/88

Shells on the Beach

You see them under palm trees on the sands
With glasses in their hands.
The graceful woman and the older man
Appear to be enjoying a good time.
For them, enjoying a good time
Is to appear
To be enjoying a good time
Among those who are mannered and well dressed
And suitably surrounded by the best.
The understated symbols of their worth
Imply that they've inherited the earth.

Someone is taking pictures.
When they look at the pictures,
Will they be able to tell
Whether or not real people
Are living inside each shell?

11/9/88

Meaning

Something within me
Longs to know you, Lord,
And is not satisfied
With emptiness.
Without you, I am bored.
With you, the smallest thing
Holds significance
So sharp, so deep,
Its very littleness
Can make me weep.

9/5/90

Blind Man's Bluff

I spend so much time
Feeling around in the dark,
Hoping that I will blunder
Into the arms of God.

The times of silence
And the child-like self denials,
The attempts at half-understood
Varieties of prayer,
The falling down and getting up again—
All, all are intended
Somehow to help me
Fumble my way toward Him.

I believe in a Reality
Beyond my comprehension and my touch
And I want to be where He is.
I have never wanted anything as much.

4/4/80

Sunday Service

The ancient usher creaking at the door,
The well-scrubbed acolyte,
The polished floor,
The sermon, also polished,
Words arranged
Precisely as the flowers on the altar—
All would appear to come before the Lord
Decently and in order.

But what about the turmoil in the soul—
The rebel spirit, the reluctant heart?
These are not quite so easily
Scoured, arranged, subdued.
Spotless the linen—but the congregation?

Knowing our hearts, our secrets, our desires,
God asks us still
To light our spirits at His Spirit's fires
And eat and drink our fill.

8/9/81

"Love Set the Table"

Love set the table.
Love became the meal.
Love fills my heart with wonder
As I kneel.

How can Love be so loving
And be real?
I speculate . . .
And yet,
Here is the table
Set by Love,
Love's meal,
And Love Himself
Prepared
In bread and wine
To be entirely shared.

8/10/84

Here in the Presence

Quietly, quietly He comes.
The sound of shaken silver starts
To ring within our hearts.
A sweetness steals
Out of the quietness
And heals.
We are alive
With an intensity of joy
We had not dreamed.
And everything that seemed
To matter
Matters now both more and less
Here in the presence
Of His holiness

3/20/81

Rendezvous

I came five miles,
Parked the car,
Entered,
Crossed myself
And knelt.
The prayers began.

Reciting them,
I felt
That I'd done something wonderful
To come,
To kneel among the faithful,
To be here.
But oh, my Lord, my lovely One, my Dear,
What kind of distance did you come
To be with me
So present and so near?

10/3/91

Presence

Like a bell pealing,
In the high chambers
Of my heart
Your name rings clear
Jesus, Jesus, Jesus—
And I am filled with joy
To find you here,
Lord of the universe and of my life,
So powerful, so loving and so near.

8/26/90

August

Garden by Moonlight

The August garden stands
Heavy with moonlight
And the scented sound
Of crickets in the night.

Among the shadowed blossoms,
Clots of white
Show where sweet phlox
Form quiet pools of light.

Dreaming of sun and butterflies,
The tangled heap
Of blossom
Lies beneath the moon
In sleep.

8/20/86

August

August leans on the land.
We stagger with his weight—
The heaviness of heat,
The slow, rich ripening.
Brazen, tyrannical,
He was well-named for Rome.

We cower away from August
In the cool
Of lakes, caves, cellars,
Air-conditioned rooms,
Living like refugees
In darkened tombs.

Corn thrives in August,
Swaggers and grows tall.
But we?
We struggle through the days
And long for fall.

8/1/87

Tornado Watch

The storm
Toys with the house,
Nuzzling it
Like some great beast of prey.
We tremble between its paws
And feel its breath—
Warm, urgent, seeking.
We try the radio
For reassurance
Only to hear a cool voice far away
Talking of Chinese art
And Mozart's diaries.
Meanwhile, the great beast
Slobbers on the glass.
We pray
And do not sleep
And wait for night to pass.

11/16/88

Ambulance

The siren screams in pain—
Screams, screams again.
Streams of fear
Bleed across country quiet.
We pause in our pursuits—
The rabbit raises his head from the clover,
The robin ignores for a moment the worm.
I put down my pen to pray
For whoever is victim this time.
The unknown fragile form
Whose spurting agony
Has been transformed into this cry of alarm,
Casting the shadow of mortality
Across the peace of the farm.

7/26/79

In Touch

Pain fades
Like dreams.
Was it just yesterday?
Is seems so long ago
That I was filled
With sympathy and love
For all who suffer pain.
Today,
My pain is gone.
Keep me from losing touch
With those who suffer
Who still hurt so much.

1/16/89

Prayers

We pray small prayers,
Forgetting
(If we ever knew)
How big You are
And how much
You can do.

We pray dull prayers,
As if we did not believe
Or weren't aware
That You are real
And that You answer prayer.

We pray indifferent prayers
As if You had not come,
As if You were not near,
As if You did not care
About our fear.

We pray dead prayers
As if You were not there.
Creator, Savior,
Living Flame of Love,
Forgive our prayer!

7/8/88

Crossing

Prayer is the threshold of the heart.
Across the bridge,
The soul may step
Into the arms of God.

Why do we stay
Imprisoned and alone
Within the walls of self
When we can pray
And move, as lightly as a butterfly,
Into the day?

3/14/79

Oh, Bother!

Why don't You give up, God?
You know me by now—
The churning restlessness,
The worrying, and how
Tense and distracted I am.

You keep asking me
To stop fussing and play,
To relax and rejoice
And admire Your new day.
I'm busy, Lord.
I have things to do.
Like Martha, I am never through.

Yes, I know Mary chose
The better part,
Simply stopped still
And opened up her heart.
It's something I would really
Like to do
But not right now. Right now
I'm much too busy
For You.

7/5/79

Predecessors

Was it like this for them,
Those early ones
Who longed to know You better,
Love You more?
Did they, too, fear
The solitude they sought
In order to seek You?
Did they, too, tire of prayer
And yet return
Hour after hour
To the place of prayer?
And did they find You there?

3/30/88

Suspect

Why don't I trust You, Lord?
You've never sent me
Anything but good.

I take Your gifts
And listen for the tick,
Then soak them
In cold, wet suspiciousness.
I'm sure the bread is stone,
The fish, as poisonous
As any scorpion's sting.

I never seem to remember
That the men
Who ate the loaves and fishes
You had blessed
Were nourished,
Not made ill.

Why do I greet Your tenderness,
Your love for me,
With such ill will?

6/4/82

Easy Yoke

He gives us burdens of delight
And fits our yokes exactly right.
His burden's light,
His burden's light.

He is a god of love and fire
Who knows our deepest heart's desire.
He burdens us with joy, with grace
And fits them gently into place.
His longing love would see us blest.
We find His burdens fit us best.

4/23/86

Safe

Stranger
And more exciting
Than wild horses,
God stands before me,
Stops me in my tracks.

Suddenly,
I no longer need to know
Where I am going,
What will happen next.
Sufficient
That He knows.
My task to rest
Serenely in His will,
To wait His best.

10/6/87

Quest

Lots of people
Go
Back and forth,
Yon and hither,
To and fro.

Instead,
I'm busy learning
To be still
Here
On this low, blue hill.

Not only still,
But stilled
And open to God's will
And filled.

9/20/88

Preparation

Shutter my eyes, my Lord,
So I may see you.
Muffle my ears
So I may hear your voice.
Silence my busy tongue
So You may speak, Lord.
Disperse my thoughts,
Let emptiness rejoice.

3/2/79

Mute

Must we use words
For everything?
Can there not be
A silent, flaming
Leap of heart
Toward Thee?

3/3/79

Miser

Shall I store happiness like honey
And keep my golden jars of it all sealed
Until the beauty in them has congealed?
Or shall I share delight
When flames of joy sweep through me?

Sorrow may come at last
But, if I have flung all my joy away,
And have none left for it to feed upon,
Perhaps it will not stay
But go and seek some miser
Who has kept life's cupboard full,
While mine is clean, swept bare,
Purged by the ecstasy of prayer.

3/4/79

Ignited

Prayer is God's burning glass.
Through it,
We see our sins so magnified
That we can spread them out
Like tinder
Underneath the scorching rays
Of focused love.
Selfishness starts to smolder,
Greed bursts into flame,
And even pride turns ashen.
Finally,
When we have let ourselves
Be perfectly consumed by sanctity,
Only light will remain.

2/23/79

Oblation

I hope each day
To offer less to You,
Each day
By Your great love to be
Diminished
Until at last I am
So decreased by Your hand
And You, so grown in me,
That my whole offering
Is just an emptiness
For You to fill
Or not
According to Your will.

11/12/79

Peace

Content to be,
Simply to be,
To be your person
Endlessly.

6/19/79

Conversation
with a Contemplative

What were you saying?
Nothing.
Where were you going?
Nowhere.
What were you doing?
Just being.
What were you seeing?
God.
God in each other.
God in everything.
That's all.
Was that enough?
Yes.
Yes, more than enough.

10/16/87

Sharing

"Peddler, what do you have
In your pack?
What are those treasures
Piled on your back?"

"A quiet mind,
Some peace of soul,
The cheerfulness
Of one made whole,
Contentment
With my place in life,
Just simple goods—
Homemade, plain, woven.
Nothing fancy here.
But if you like them
Help yourself, my dear."

1/11/90

Blessed

My nets are breaking, Lord
I had not thought
To catch such an abundance
Of your love.
So many years
I've toiled in my own strength
And taken nothing.

Now, suddenly, I'm filled
With you, Your love,
Your goodness, mercy, might.
You are my Lord, my love,
Who gives me all delight.

4/19/86

Vocation

The thing is that
You don't just give things up
In one great gesture
So you're done with it.
You learn to die
As He did,
Willingly.
You fall a lot
But keep on getting up
And going on.

It's better
If you take
One day
Or just one minute
At a time
And don't make promises
That you can't keep.
And better,
When you fall,
If you can laugh
As well as weep.

2/25/87

Offering

The only thing I have
To offer, Lord,
Is me,
And I don't know
Quite who
Or what I am.
Everything I can give
Is only what You first
Have given me—
Health, strength, intelligence,
The power to love.
Please take
From one small bit
Of holy dust
Praise and thanksgiving,
Love and joy and trust.

9/5/87

Clay

Lord, we are clay,
Essential clay, mere earth.
Dying, we will
Become again
The substance of our birth.

As you used clay
To heal the blind man's eyes,
Mix Your grace and Your power
With our clay,
So when we kneel,
We will arise
Transformed,
So you can use the clay of us
To heal.

5/9/91

Bridge

Clinging to heaven
By my fingertips,
My being racked
With my desire for God,
I am become
A ladder swaying,
Stretched, precarious,
'Twixt heaven and earth.

Make me submissive, Lord,
Open to Thee
And willing to be used.
May someone
Find in me,
By thy great grace,
A means of reaching Thee.

6/7/86

Prayer

Dear Lord,
Add my small drop
Of prayer
To the cool cup of grace
You offer
This parched soul.
May he drink deep
And find himself
Made whole.

5/9/87

Blessings

My rising prayers for you,
Ascending, meet
Your prayers for me
Mounting before His seat
And intermingle there,
Their beauty blending.

Our prayers of love
And His love, coalescing,
Create a single strand
Of joy and blessing
With which He garlands us.

Glorified by this love,
We go our ways
Among the ordinary moments
Of our days.

2/24/88

Homebody

I stay at home,
Cannot go out,
But all my prayers
Go round about.

This one is blessed,
That one is healed.
What God will do
Is not revealed
To me.
I just stay home
And pray.
God does the rest
In His own way.

1/1/88

Weary

Dear Lord,
You know how tired I am.
I couldn't muster up
A pious feeling now
For anyone.
You know I love You, Lord.
The love and the committed will
Are there,
Firmly in place
Beneath all this fatigue.
But, Lord, I'm tired.
Thank You for loving me
Just as I am
And telling me
That I can rest in You.
I will. I do.

4/21/86

Bishop

As plump and purple as a finch,
The bishop stood before us all
And prayed
Serene, compassionate and unafraid.
His, like the finch's,
Was a cheerful song—
That God, who made us,
Loves us still
And comes to tell us so
And ever will.

9/19/84

Epitaph

I hope it will be said
When I am dead,
"She wrote good poems
And she made good bread."

But let it not be said
Till I am dead.
To say it now
Would surely turn my head.

1/23/78